The Journey

The Journey

ARNOLD M. PATENT

Celebration Publishing
Tucson, Arizona

Celebration Publishing
230 South Palace Gardens Drive
Tucson, AZ 85748

Cover illustration by Selma Patent
Text and cover design by Kaelin Chappell

Library of Congress Control Number 2002103847
ISBN 0-9708081-1-9

First Printing April 2002
Printed in the United States of America

To my spiritual coach

Grady Claire Porter

with love and appreciation

ACKNOWLEDGMENTS

Selma for being the perfect wife,
friend and partner

Betty and Frank McElhill for
their generous support

Elton Lewis for creating and
managing a beautiful website

Kaelin Chappell for enhancing
the spirit of the book with her designs

CONTENTS

Seeing Clearly

The Journey Continues

Appendix

INTRODUCTION

I have spent the last 20 years trying to understand the game we call *life*. The process began with the insights that came as I sought to clarify what had been so confusing.

After sharing these insights informally with friends and acquaintances, I was invited to present them on a more formal basis, first in living rooms and then in larger public venues. Many of the details of the early years of this experience are contained in my first book, *You Can Have It All*.

Staying conscious of these insights, or using the always-available distractions to divert my attention is my choice. I have noticed that as I heighten my awareness, the insights multiply as well as the support to more deeply accept and appreciate the process. My awe of the way I am being supported encourages me to deepen my commitment to continue. I am grateful that my commitment to expand my awareness is always matched by an increase in the level of support offered to me. This support has taken the form of one-on-one coaching.

I have kept extensive handwritten notes of the coaching experience knowing that one day I would report these experiences in a book. One morning I awoke to the realization that I could best tell the story by giving the reader as much information as possible including my personal experiences. Appreciating how enjoyable this approach would be for me, I could not wait to begin.

The
Journey
Begins

CHAPTER 1

A New Perspective

Oneness

I am One with everything. All that I see is me. The words are simple and straightforward. Yet the elusiveness of this concept as I have attempted to grasp it is almost painful. Upon reflection, I can see the reasons I resist accepting this idea.

Who wants to be one with poverty, crime, disease and terrorism? Who wants to be one with fear, anger, frustration, depression and shame? As a practical matter, I was not ready to begin to accept the concept of Oneness, or any of the other Universal Principles, until I was willing to recognize, at least intellectually, that these disagreeable conditions and uncomfortable feelings are based on how I see them and what I call them.

The Importance of Our Perspective

The gap between the natural state of the Universe and the way the world in which we live *appears to us* seems insurmountable until we see the true relationship between them. Instead of being far apart, these states are very closely related. In fact, they are just different phases of a continuing journey.

The journey begins when, as our Soul Self, all that we know is our true state of being. Our experience is only of harmony, peace, unconditional love and infinite abundance. We identify as the God Presence (Power of God). Eager to experience and express this Power in all situations and circumstances, the Soul Self initiates an exploration of ourselves as humans.

Intentional Amnesia

In order for this exploration to be meaningful, we have to give up memory of who we really are, and what our natural state is. There is no way that we can accept feeling powerless, angry or mean-spirited if we retain awareness of the God Presence.

It Takes The God Presence

Who other than the God Presence (our Soul Self) could possibly create the complexity and intensity of experiences we have endured: Hitler and Mother Theresa, atomic bombs and peace marches, anger and retaliation, forgiveness and acceptance.

We have given ourselves many lifetimes of extraordinary experiences. During this time, our awareness has expanded and with it our perspective. We are now ready to enter the next phase of our journey.

CHAPTER 2

Two Phases—
An Introduction

Phase One

For simplicity sake, we can divide our lifetime into two phases. The first phase encompasses the period during which we cleverly hide our power by filling our consciousness with beliefs in limitation and powerlessness that make it seem that:

1. we are at the effect of events and circumstances, and

2. the Universe and all in It are often our uncaring nemeses rather than our loving supporters.

This is the phase during which our participation in these events and circumstances justify feelings we call fear, pain, grief, loss and abandonment. Although we often wish this phase would disappear, like a bad dream, it contains valuable information for the next phase of our journey: the map of places where we have hidden our power.

In the absence of reclaiming our power, we continue to experience the reflection of the limited beliefs that remain planted in our consciousness. Keeping our power hidden takes great effort. The power is enormous and is constantly pushing its way toward freedom. Much of the discomfort we feel is the impact of this internal conflict.

Why Hide the Power

We hide the power of our Soul Self (the God Presence) so that we can explore the trials and tribulations that we encounter as human beings. After hiding all this power, we can easily accept beliefs that we are unloved and unsupported in an uncaring and hostile world, and are at the effect of circumstances in our lives from economic conditions and terrorism to our own fears and angers.

Hiding our power is the other side of the coin of giving up memory of who we really are. And both are prerequisites for our journey as human beings.

Hiding Our Power

With the support and guidance of our Soul Self, we hide our power in places we tell ourselves to avoid—situations, beliefs and feelings that we find uncomfortable and distasteful, such as failure, illness, fear and shame. Our Soul Self then helps us to keep the power hidden by installing a gatekeeper that we can call the Protector. The mission given this part of us is to do whatever it takes to keep us away from our power.

The Protector is diligent and resourceful. Every time we get close to our power, this guardian of the hiding places finds a way to send us elsewhere. From many years of experience, the Protector knows the most effective ways to misdirect us. Memory lapses, self-doubt and avoidance of discomfort are just some of the patterns that the Protector relies on to carry out the mission assigned to It.

Phase Two

Finding Our Power

When we begin the process of looking for our power, we need to be mindful of the strategies we have employed to deter us. However, we cannot treat these strategies as obstacles to overcome. Rather, we can utilize these same strategies to find our power.

Seeing part of us as creating obstacles for other parts keeps alive the sensation of inner conflict that was one of the strategies we employed to keep the power hidden. The approach that works for me is creating harmony within, bringing all parts of me together in support of my new intention.

I create this harmony by acknowledging and appreciating the parts of me that have brilliantly hidden my power and keep me away from it so that I can have the experiences I have come here to have. In other words, I see the creation of apparent conflict within me as purposeful. Then, I focus on the fact that I am not really at conflict with my Self. I have used my power to create the illusion of conflict.

Our Soul is always aware of who we really are. The challenge we face is accepting that truth and having it become real for us. We are looking to bring the Soul's awareness into our human awareness.

As we build our acknowledgment and appreciation for what it takes to hide our power, and keep it hidden, we are verifying for ourselves that our intention to proceed is real. We are also demonstrating to the Protector that we have truly changed our intention from one of hiding our power to that of finding it. As soon as that intention reaches 100%, the Protector becomes our ally in showing us where the power is hidden, and supports us in reclaiming it.

CHAPTER 3

&

Getting Ready

Intention

In order to understand the presence of any current experience, we first look at universal mathematics. This is mathematics in its simplest form. All that we need to remember is 0% and 100%. Anything less than 100% equals 0%.

Whatever situation we are facing is present because our intention to have that precise experience is 100%. When we look to open the energy around any present experience, our intention to do so must first reach 100%. Otherwise, no movement occurs.

Nonjudgment

I know the Principle of nonjudgment: Whenever I judge anyone or anything, my experience with that person or situation remains the way I see it. The release of the judgment frees the energy so that I may expand my view of the person or situation.

I now see judgment as a vital piece of information to lead me to the places where I have hidden my power. When what I see or feel is less than perfect, I know I have located a hiding place for my power.

Next, I acknowledge and appreciate my acceptance of the judgment and all other aspects of the situation. Then I embrace all aspects of the situation in unconditional love and appreciation.

Loving Ourselves

Everything I experience is colored by the way I feel about myself. When I feel less than unconditionally loving and accepting of myself, I see and feel the world around me in the same way. This is true since I am the whole of the Universe, and there is nothing outside of me.

How I feel about myself is determined by my beliefs. As a way of providing me with the best possible support, the Universe makes certain that every belief I hold is reflected back to me as though I am surrounded by 360 degrees of mirrors. I am always seeing and feeling a reflection of the state of my own consciousness. I am constantly living the drama that is the playing out of my beliefs.

This is a huge gift that the Universe presents to me. Accepting this gift means a willingness to acknowledge that every opinion I hold, every anger I express, and every circumstance I find repugnant is the way I see or feel about myself.

A common belief that I have accepted is that I am not perfect just the way I am. As long as I hold that belief, I cannot possibly love myself unconditionally. Until I love myself just the way I am, I cloud my view of our unconditionally loving and supportive Universe.

Nothing Outside Ourselves

I pay close attention to any situation that causes me discomfort, since I know I have located a place where I have hidden some power. This focus supports me in opening the energy in the beliefs that I am not perfect just the way I am, and that there are events and circumstances that are more powerful than I am. Examples of beliefs I have opened, or am continuing to open, are the reality of disease, failure, shame, deceit, pain, working for a living and death. Opening the energy in these beliefs is a way I expand my capacity to appreciate that I am the whole of the Universe and that there is nothing outside of me.

Our Emotions

Love is the only energy in the Universe and joy is the only true feeling. Fear, shame, deceit, distrust and anger are names we have given to feelings to help us hide our power. We use the events in our lives to deepen these emotions, creating additional layers of separation between our human selves and our power. This also creates a greater distance between our human selves and our joyfulness.

When we revisit these hiding places for the purpose of reclaiming our power, we remove the labels we have placed on these energies. They are, when free of the labels we have assigned to them, a broad array of feeling qualities. The range of these feelings is no different from the vast pallet of colors available to an artist, or the infinite variety of harmonics available to a composer. These feelings are the God Presence —an indescribable richness and forever expanding beauty of joy.

The
Phases

CHAPTER 4

ༀ

Phase I

Let's look at our lives as though we are characters in a play. This play is written before we are born under the guidance of our Soul Self. Each individual play is part of a larger play and each role is crafted to be in support of all other roles.

Each participant is a volunteer who knows that all the support that is needed to play the role is provided in advance. At this formative stage, every participant knows who he really is and what it takes to have the play seem like a real experience.

We know the perfect family, culture, community, events and circumstances that will give us the experiences we choose to have. We know the beliefs to accept that support us in hiding our power so that the play follows the script.

Once we are born, all that we come here to explore begins to unfold. We take on all the beliefs opposite to who we are and what the natural state of the Universe is.

With our Soul Self's support, we proceed to hide our power in places we are least likely to look; and, we assign a part of ourselves the role of the Protector of those hiding places with the job assignment to do whatever it takes to block our entry.

The play continues with the building of the illusion of how powerless we are, and how much we are at the effect of forces in the world around us. We accept the reality of such illusions as struggle, danger and failure. We funnel feelings into these beliefs creating intense emotional states such as fear and shame, which serve to keep us away from the places where we hide our power.

We tell ourselves that we are not acceptable just the way we are, and set up conditions we must comply with, such as working hard and pleasing others, before we are entitled to feel good about ourselves. We also learn to interpret expressions such as anger, sadness, fear and shame as devoid of love. These conditions and interpretations become additional hiding places for our power.

CHAPTER 5

⤳

Phase II

Part One

The awakening begins:

The awareness emerges that there is more to life than struggle and pain, and that we are not as helpless as we once thought.

Our hearts open more.

The Universe begins to appear as a loving and supportive presence.

We begin to feel more powerful and less at the effect of forces outside of ourselves.

We see life less as adversarial and competitive and more as mutually supportive.

The contrast between how we are accustomed to see the world and the new way it appears becomes more obvious.

We find ourselves fluctuating between these two worlds and not totally comfortable in either.

As we expand our trust in this new way, we notice that there is a part of us that resists our forward movement; the more deeply we try to trust, the harder it becomes for us to do so. The Protector is still doing what we have instructed It to do.

This leads us to the awareness that in order to enroll the Protector in support of our new vision, we must first convince It we are truly committed to do whatever we must to accept who we really are, and what we know the Universe really is. The next phase of the journey is about to begin.

Part Two

The awakening continues:

The beliefs that support our limited view of life become more evident, as they present themselves in our daily activities.

We realize we have set up very powerful mechanisms to keep the limited view in place.

We enroll the Protector's support to help us find the places where our power is hidden.

We accept more of our power.

We are willing to see more of our lives as a reflection of what we believe.

We begin to recognize that everything is supportive of us.

We appreciate our power.

We focus on expanding the flow of energy (power) through us.

We encourage the emergence of our Soul Self.

What our Soul Self knows:

Our power is our joy, abundance, peace, divinity, perfection, trust, gratitude, generosity, creativity, inspiration and unconditional love.

Our purpose is experiencing and expressing the Power of God.

We are perfect in every situation just the way we are.

Everything keeps expanding including the richness of abundance.

Abundance is unconditional; we accept and appreciate as much as we wish.

The more we savor each moment that seems worthy of savoring, the more moments we find to savor, until every moment seems worthy of savoring. This is the way we enjoy our natural state of abundance.

There are no mistakes or accidents.

We are all volunteers. We each have a specific role to play. We are all perfectly prepared for our roles.

Every event is an accurate reflection of the state of our consciousness. These events reveal our limited beliefs that are the hiding places for our power. The more committed we are to uncovering these beliefs, the more support the Universe provides us to see them clearly.

Nothing in our physical world has any power; all power resides in us.

Each of us is the whole of the Universe.

Each of us is the Power of God. We are all One.

When we really know and trust that we are each the Power of God, our lives become a joyful game.

Abundance

CHAPTER 6

⌇

What Is Abundance?

What is abundance?

Abundance is the free, full and unfettered flow of the Divine Energy of who we really are. We express and experience true abundance as we acknowledge, accept and appreciate this limitless identity.

What are the Principles underlying abundance?

1. We are all imbued with the full power of the Universe to experience and express in our own unique ways.

2. All of us are provided with the perfect support to live life abundantly in accordance with our purpose for being here.

3. Each of us is whole and complete and nothing can be taken from us. Who would, and why would they?

4. Whatever is present in our lives is the perfect support, and is a gift from the Universe.

5. Expressing ourselves fully and freely is a gift to the Universe and all in It.

6. We are all equal.

7. The Universe and all in It are constantly showering us with love and support.

8. We can join in mutual support to expand our acceptance of abundance. We do this by accepting and appreciating ourselves just the way we are.

9. The outcome of trusting the Universe is the miracle.

CHAPTER 7

☙

Procedure for Reclaiming Our Power

We remind ourselves:

1. the gift the Universe is bringing 45

places us right where we have hidden our power,

2. to stay in the fullness of that energy just the way it is, no matter how uncomfortable the feeling,

3. the more uncomfortable the feeling, the more power we have located,

4. to let go of any description we have of the energy such as fear, shame, anger or discouragement,

5. to open our hearts and embrace the fullness of the energy,

6. to feel appreciation for all participants in the drama,

7. to feel appreciation for the Universe in bringing us

this gift,

8. to feel appreciation for ourselves for accepting the gift,

9. to feel appreciation that we are always in the fullness of our power.

CHAPTER 8

⋄

Avoiding Abundance

Limitation

Creating the concept of limitation is a brilliant way to hide the power contained in our natural state of abundance. I chose to explore this concept in many ways. One way in particular seems worth sharing—paying less for something is better than paying more.

I did not fully appreciate the extent to which I had resisted the flow of abundance until I started the process of opening the energy in my many beliefs in limitation. That is when I realized that by limiting what I am willing to give, I am also limiting what I am willing to receive. Giving and receiving are always in balance.

Knowing that there is no limit to the flow of abundance, I now receive gratefully and give generously. Opening the flow of abundance is a huge gift I have accepted from the Universe. Accepting this gift expresses itself for the benefit of all with whom I interact.

Conditionality

Our lives are filled with conditions. We are taught that unless we meet these conditions, love and support is withheld from us. First at home, then at school and finally in the workplace, we are trained to behave in prescribed ways so that we are accepted. Our freedom to experience and express ourselves, and thus our feeling of empowerment, is continually diminished. This is part of the process of hiding our power.

Accepting abundance as our natural state means:

1. paying attention to the conditions we believe to be true as they surface,

2. reminding ourselves that our acceptance of these conditions is intentional and purposeful,

3. embracing the conditions, and ourselves for accepting them, as the way to free the power hidden in the conditions,

4. feeling the increased richness and value of the flow of power through us as our acceptance of abundance,

5. feeling the increased richness and value of the flow of love through us as acceptance of our magnificence just the way we are.

CHAPTER 9

⟳

The Present Moment

A Law of the Universe is that everything occurs in the present moment. This means that the full power of the Universe resides in the present moment. This also means that the fullness of our power as the God Presence resides in the present moment.

Our perception of linear time is just a disguise we create to hide our power. We make believe that we can separate ourselves from an event or circumstance that is uncomfortable.

Placing my attention fully in the present moment, and accepting everything as part of the present moment is a lot easier said than done. However, it is a part of the puzzle that I am piecing together.

A related Principle is that everything is perfect just the way it is. Putting the two Principles together, we have the perfection of what is, just the way it is, in each present moment. What follows is the acceptance and appreciation of these truths.

Let's look at an aspect of my life as an example. I grew up with the belief that it is my responsibility to provide well for my wife and myself during our lifetimes by having investment income sufficient to meet that responsibility. I also grew up believing that a pain-free body is better than one with pain.

The truth is that right now my life is just fine. However, a financial projection into the future based on what I see now, and mood swings and physical discomfort, provide reasons why everything is not fine.

When I remove the beliefs and projections, and accept what is as perfect, it becomes that. To gain this clarity, I step back from these situations and look at them as the God Presence that I am. Then, I ask myself, "If God were having any of these experiences that I consider less than ideal, would I worry that God is making a poor choice, or that She is in over Her head?" This approach reminds me that I can trust that God is having the precise experiences that She wishes to have, and that all is in divine order.

This approach also reminds me that I am free to choose to see everything that occurs as perfect, just the way it is, and, with my heart fully open, accept each moment as a gift from the Universe. Often, the gift is what I see that initially seems less than perfect. I am opening to a broader view of my Soul Self, not what I consider an ideal event or circumstance.

Rather than fixing a situation that appears unsatisfactory or even horrendous, I am accepting the perfection of everything just the way it is. When I do this, there is no issue about the amount of money I may have available for some day in the future. There is no consideration of how else I could feel.

Am I really concerned about living on very little money?

No. My concern is about the shame of not meeting a standard originally set by the culture in which I grew up, but that I have adopted as my own.

In directing my attention to the feelings of shame and fear of failure, the Universe offers me a gift: showing me places where I have hidden my power. I accept the gift by reminding myself that what I have been calling shame and fear of failure are just disguises for my power as a God Presence.

After much practice, I have come to appreciate that failure is just a belief in my own mind. I know that I only see failure reflected from others as long as that belief is present in me. And if I do, the Universe is giving me the gift of showing me where I still have hidden some power.

CHAPTER 10

✺

Perceptual Reality and the Mirror Principle

Abundance is present in my life. The same is true of harmony, peace, freedom and joy. Fear, shame and limitation are disguises I create in consciousness to cloud the view of my true Presence.

The Mirror Principle and state of consciousness go together. I am always looking at a reflection of my own consciousness. If I believe in limitation of any sort, I see that limitation reflected back to me in my daily life.

For example: When I perceive that something like a loaf of bread is not already mine, I assume that to obtain it I have to pay for it. When I know that the bread is already mine, I accept the gift; in the spirit of generosity and appreciation, I make a gift in return.

Feeling gratitude for a gift is natural to me, as is giving generously. I have learned how to see and feel limitation of all sorts with great intention; opening the energy in what I believe requires equal intention.

The Mirror Principle is the constant reminder of my acceptance of beliefs that the Universe is less than totally abundant; I am less than totally powerful; and I am not loved unconditionally by all. When I perceive myself as a failure, the circumstances in my life appear to back me up. I am free to make a case for anything that I choose to believe.

The self-supportive approach I use is to keep in consciousness how abundant the Universe is, and how powerful I am while I am feeling unsupported, unimportant and powerless. Correspondingly, I support those people who see themselves as failures by feeling compassion for them while I remember how powerful they really are.

I cannot truly support people without opening my heart to appreciate their feelings. However, I know that I am no support to them if I accept their interpretation of themselves as powerless and their feelings as other than loving.

We live our lives in accordance with an agreement we make before we come here. All that we need to live that way is given to us. Being homeless is not a sign of failure. Being a millionaire is not a sign of success.

I am committed to be present in each moment of my life and to accept that moment as perfect just the way it is. In this way, I expand my awareness and experience of the absolute abundance that I am. The more I open to each present moment and embrace it as a wonderful gift, the more magnificent that moment becomes, the more energized I feel, and the more open I am to accept the limitless abundance of our loving and supportive Universe. I also eagerly share these gifts with all who come into my presence.

CHAPTER 11

Opening to Abundance

Doing What We Love
and Acceptance of Abundance

As naturally powerful beings, there is no better way to promote the flow of that power than by creatively expressing our talents for the sheer joy of generously sharing our gift.

Where does the support to sustain ourselves come from when we do what we love for the sheer joy of doing it? That support, which is felt as the flow of Universal power through us, comes in direct proportion to our unconditional acceptance of the gift of abundance. What are some of the ways we accept abundance?

1. knowing how powerful we are,

2. knowing how valuable we are,

3. knowing how valuable our gift is,

4. knowing how loving and supportive the Universe and all in It are,

5. knowing how generous we are,

6. knowing how appreciative we are,

7. knowing how infinite abundance is.

Trust in the Abundance

The richness, the fullness and the power of the love and support of the Universe are all incorporated in what we refer to as abundance. Living in this abundance is completely natural to us, and is a gift from the Universe for us to accept, appreciate and then share generously. This is our true support.

Placing our trust in the abundance means opening ourselves to the flow of the power of the Universe through us. Having set up conditions for our qualification as divine beings, we have made believe that we are cut off from our divine birthright. The opportunity we have is to support each other in accepting and appreciating what is already ours.

Abundance Is A Gift

What does accepting abundance really mean? The answer is the willingness to see everything in our lives as a gift of unconditional love and support flowing to us from the Universe. The conditions we place on these gifts are the ways we avoid accepting the flow of this unconditional love and support. Whatever transpires during the day that we do not consider a gift is a way that we resist the flow of abundance.

Another aspect of accepting abundance is determining the value of the flow of these gifts. The value we place on this flow is a measure of the value we place on ourselves, as well as a measure of the amount of richness we are willing to receive.

There is no limit to our value or the richness of abundance available to us. Together we can support each other in accepting an ever-increasing flow of abundance. There is also no limit to how much fun we can have in playing together in mutual support and generously sharing our abundance.

Seeing
Clearly

CHAPTER 12

⤳

Accepting the Gifts

Everything that I see and feel is a reflection of the state of my consciousness. Taking advantage of this extraordinary gift is up to me.

Why would anyone overlook or avoid this gift? The answer is simple and obvious. Much of what we see is uncomfortable, and we believe that looking at it more closely will add to our discomfort.

This is proof of how brilliantly we not only hide our power, but also keep ourselves from going near it. However, the same brilliance is available to us in uncovering the disguises and opening ourselves to the power. That brilliant part of us is our Soul Self, the part that sees clearly what is being reflected in the events of our day.

When I expressed my willingness to open to this level of support, the Universe provided it in the form of a spiritual coach. This intermediary hears and sees, with clarity, the information my Soul Self is communicating to me. With practice, I have learned to see and hear the messages myself.

There is no limit to the unconditional love, support and abundance that the Universe offers us. There is also no limit to how much of this unconditional love, support and abundance we can accept, appreciate and share.

Progress

Every time I open a belief, I free myself from the sense of limitation contained in the belief, and I am now present in a new reality. We do not regress to positions that we have outgrown. What may seem like a fallback is just the return of what is left of the belief for further opening.

Every time I open a belief, I feel more peacefulness, harmony, abundance and joy—my Soul's natural state sitting under layers of beliefs I purposely accepted as the first part of my journey into the human experience. I trust that this opening process is a progression from living in the human as a human experience to living in the human as a Soul experience.

Trust

The beliefs I have intentionally and purposefully accepted as true become the lens through which I see life. I am not only accustomed to this way of seeing—I rely on it. I have accepted beliefs that some behaviors are good and others are bad, that viruses cause illnesses, and that some people are strong and others are weak.

As I proceed on my journey to open these beliefs, I exercise great patience and perseverance. I trust in my wholeness, completeness and power, and I also trust that the Universe is unconditionally loving and supportive at all times and under all circumstances. Maintaining this trust is the way I stay committed to continue with the process of opening myself to who I really am.

Beliefs and Knowing

Our conscious minds use our creativity to make up beliefs that give rise to the circumstances we have come into the human to explore. When we are ready to open these beliefs, our Souls guide us through the process, selecting the ones we are ready to open. The discomforts we feel are evidence of the beliefs we have not yet opened.

Every opening of a belief brings us closer to our knowing, which is our consciousness free of the sense of limitation contained in our beliefs. As stated previously, we do not retreat to positions we have outgrown. Once we open a belief, our greater clarity becomes a new platform from which we move to even greater clarity and knowing.

Our natural state is a consciousness free of beliefs: a state of total freedom, joy, abundance, harmony and peace. *That state is always present, patiently awaiting our full acceptance and appreciation.*

CHAPTER 13

◦

Removing the Veils

Events and Circumstances

In Phase One, the events and circumstances of our lives are contrivances we use to support us in engaging in the experiences we came here to explore. In Phase Two, they lead us to the places where our power is hidden. Other than as vehicles for the above-stated purposes, these events and circumstances are of no importance. The closer we come to accepting who we really are, the more readily we can accept their inherent insignificance.

When we attempt to make an event or circumstance more to our liking, such as earning more money or finding a more comfortable employment, we are, in effect, trying to change the mirror so that it reflects a more satisfactory image. The image we see is the perfect reflection of what we believe. By using the mirror to guide us in opening beliefs, the same events and circumstances, when seen without the veil of the beliefs, appear as perfect just the way they are.

Reflections

Each of us is in perfect support of all others. We offer this perfect support by reflecting accurately the state of consciousness of those with whom we interact. We are all volunteers; no one is a victim or a perpetrator.

Horrific and seemingly unjustifiable acts are wake-up calls to deep truths that we are ready to face: no one really dies; we are each whole and complete and nothing can be taken from us; we are all part of one experience; we are each having the precise experience we have come into the human to have; and most important of all—love is the only energy in the Universe. Whenever we see other than love, our vision is clouded by a belief. The dramatic event is the reminder that we can see with greater clarity when we are willing.

Loving Ourselves Unconditionally

I project the way I feel about myself upon the world. This is true since I am the whole of the Universe. Opening my beliefs to see with greater clarity is also opening to feel more love for myself.

The reasons I give myself for not being worthy of unconditional love are all beliefs that I have intentionally accepted. The closets in my mind are filled with these reasons. I can quickly find justification for withholding love from myself. I can just as quickly open to greater acceptance and love for myself just the way I am.

Self-Validation

Self-validation means accepting, appreciating and loving myself unconditionally as whole and complete just the way I am. The signal that I have not reached that place is when I look for someone or something for validation. Seeking awards, recognition and endorsements are examples of attempts I have used to fill the void of self-acceptance and self-love.

Only I can validate myself. The Universe in Its infinite wisdom and constant love and support for me keeps reminding me of the presence of this void as a way of encouraging me to fill it. There is no greater gift I can grant myself than opening my heart to feel this love for myself.

There is Nothing Outside of Us

This is such an important concept that I am calling attention to it once again. Many of the beliefs in the collective consciousness relate to events, people and substances that have the capacity to bring us harm, take something from us or bring us pain: viruses, terrorists and economic conditions, to name but a few on a seemingly endless list.

The acceptance of these beliefs is what we came here to do. However, that is just the first part of our journey into the human. The next part is opening these beliefs so that we return to the knowing that we are the God Presence, whole and complete just the way we are from whom nothing can be taken.

Removing the veil that clouds the view of our God Presence is seeing and feeling through our open hearts. When our hearts are open, we know that all is love, that we are whole and complete, and that nothing can be taken from us. Giving and receiving love from the fullness of who we are is our natural way of relating, and there is no limit to how generously we can give that love or how much gratitude we can feel when we receive it

A Vision of Reality

Beyond our physical presence is our true entity, the God Presence in all Its divine glory. The power, beauty, magnificence, joy and abundance of this Presence awaits our full recognition, acceptance and appreciation. Take a few minutes to close your eyes and visualize this Presence. Feel the richness and fullness of this Presence. Use this vision and feeling as your new point of reference for who you are. See and feel the events and circumstances of your life as a game you, as a God Presence, came here to play and enjoy. See the participants in this game as your support to remember who each of you really are. And have fun!

The
Journey
Continues

CHAPTER 14

꩜

Playing the Game

There is general agreement in our society that pain, aging and working for a living are all a normal part of life.

Viewed from the broader perspective presented in previous chapters, we can see that each of these concepts is a collection of beliefs that are perfect hiding places for our power. What makes the game of life so interesting is that each of our beliefs has a unique quality that is very personal to each of us. By examining these beliefs, we gain appreciation for the extraordinary accomplishment of hiding our power so that we can have the experiences that seem so real to us.

Pain

Pain is a great hiding place for our power. Since opening the energy in a belief requires us to feel the energy we have hidden, labeling something as pain is an ingenious way to make certain we avoid going near that hiding place.

The first step in approaching pain is being clear that this characterization of the energy is something we cleverly contrive. We are responding to the label, which is not what the energy really is. All energy is love—the Power of God—that we are experiencing and expressing.

After being clear on the first step, make a list of your personal beliefs about pain. Then, taking one belief at a time, review the earlier chapters while keeping that belief in mind. This will heighten your awareness to the reflections you are receiving that tell you how that belief is clouding your clarity that you are the Power of God.

Every thought, action, feeling, event and circumstance in our lives tells us what we believe. All that is required of us is to pay attention to and appreciate the enormous gift that we are receiving.

Aging

Our acceptance of this concept is reinforced daily as we watch people age and then die. Many of us look to postpone aging by exercise and using products that we hope will retard or reverse the process. This approach is similar to the use of drugs to dull or eliminate the symptom of pain. In both of these examples we are looking to something outside of us for help. Acceptance of this approach reinforces in our consciousness the belief that there is power outside of us. If you wish to open the energy in your beliefs about aging, follow the suggestions given for pain.

Working for a Living

Disguising the truth that abundance is the natural state of the Universe and the natural state of each of us is not easy.

However, our determined acceptance of the concept of "working for a living" is a tribute to our creativity, ingenuity and commitment to keep our natural state hidden.

We are *beings* not *doings*. Our lives don't *work* or *not work*. Our lives *are* just the way they are. Our appreciation for being who we are—the Power of God—helps us open the energy around the belief that we are required to *do* something. The more we just open to receive and appreciate whatever is in our lives in the present moment, the more we realize the difference between *doing* and *being*.

In preparing to open the belief in "working for a living," it is helpful to remember that you have available all of the creativity, ingenuity and commitment that you used to accept that belief. If you wish to open the energy in the belief that you must work for a living, follow the suggestions given above.

Supporting Each Other

Many years ago, as a way of practicing the Universal Principles that I offer in my seminars and books, a particular model of support called the Mutual Support Group was created. A handbook was developed to provide guidelines and exercises for these meetings. The appendix of this book contains a revision of that handbook designed to support those who wish to join together to help each other expand the process of opening the energy around their beliefs. Only two people are required to start a group. Before starting such a group, be clear that the meeting is not for advice giving or discussions. The sole purpose is to avail ourselves of the power of mutual support.

CHAPTER 15

✑

My Own Experiences

As mentioned previously, we all have gone to great lengths to hide our enormous power so that we can explore our lives as human beings. Five personal examples illustrate ways I have hidden my power, as well as the ways I am removing the disguises to open this energy.

Gratitude

We are all naturally grateful for the love and support that is constantly showered upon us by the Universe and all in It. Hiding this energy of gratitude and keeping it hidden is not easy. For a long time I have been feeling more gratitude for many of the events and circumstances that I feel good about. However, I was aware that there was still a great deal of gratitude that I was hiding.

My spiritual coach suggested that I feel gratitude for myself for how resourceful I have been in hiding my power.

This helps me focus on the part of the process that I had overlooked.

My mind tells me that I am beyond the hiding phase and into the opening phase. But just opening the energy in the beliefs I have created to hide my power, overlooks the energy still hidden in the ingenuity and cleverness that I use to hide the power and keep it hidden.

Feeling gratitude for myself in accomplishing this difficult job has led to an increase in the amount of gratitude I am able to feel. I have also noticed that in searching out the clever ways I have hidden the power, I have located new places where power is hidden.

Generosity

We all have a natural desire to be generous. As I have heightened my awareness to ways I am withholding my generosity, I have located beliefs I have created to keep me away from that source of power. Many of these beliefs reflect a basic inner conflict: fear of being successful as showing too much power, and fear of not being successful and therefore not meeting cultural and family expectations. Other related beliefs include: having to work hard to earn anything worthwhile, and having to conserve what I earn to support my wife and myself in later years. These beliefs reinforce a general belief in limitation and make feeling generous difficult for me.

In addition to opening the energy in these beliefs, I feel appreciation for myself for how cleverly I have hidden my feelings of generosity. This serves to both deepen my feelings of generosity along with my feelings of gratitude.

I have gained a great appreciation for how committed we

all are to stretch the bounds of believability and drama that characterize life as a human being. This has deepened my feelings of compassion for everyone.

Obligation

When we look at the concept of obligation, we can sense the great lengths we have had to go to hide the enormous power contained in our natural feelings of generosity and gratitude. Our beliefs in obligation are staggering. Cultural and legal demands pervade our society. There are family obligations such as those demanded of parents to children, spouses to each other, children to parents and to teachers. Then there are obligations of all citizens to law enforcement officials. In addition, there are obligations to pay taxes.

I have accepted these beliefs. I took on a huge sense of obligation to comply with family expectations as a child — being a son who made his parents proud all the way to becoming a lawyer. I have been meticulously law abiding, and served time in the army to meet governmental obligations.

Perceiving my compliance in all of these instances as involuntary and burdensome, I built up a great deal of resentment toward my parents, the educational establishment and the government. Keeping the sense of obligation and resentment alive has helped me to hide a lot of my power. After many years under the burden of these feelings, I have spent many years opening the energy around the beliefs that led to these feelings. My current relationship with family members and the government is one of continually freeing myself and them from any sense of obligation. I voluntarily choose to receive from and give support to family members and the government.

There is another aspect of obligation that is worth mentioning—the concept of debt. This is a mirror of our obligation consciousness. The size of these debts is indicative of the amount of power we have hidden in this concept. (Our individual, corporate and government debt has grown to trillions of dollars.)

I participated in this vast endeavor by taking on various debts from personal and business loans to personal and business mortgages. As part of accepting the belief in debts, I used as my model the behavior of the so-called financial sophisticate—the person who withholds payment of his bills to the last minute, using the withheld funds to earn interest. After spending many years feeling the discomfort of playing the debt game in this way, I have committed myself to open the energy around my beliefs in obligation and debt. Instead of withholding payments as long as possible, I allow myself the joy of paying the bills as soon as they come in. I also enjoy the simplicity and ease of having no debts. This is not because having debts is bad or wrong. Borrowing money can be a fun experience, provided it is done with appreciation— enjoying the giving and receiving of a loving energy.

The pervasiveness of obligation and debt as a burdensome experience makes it very easy to find places to practice feeling gratitude for our ingenuity and dedication to hide so much of our power in these concepts. I continue with this practice in support of opening the immense amount of power hidden in our obligation and debt consciousness.

September 11, 2001

At ten minutes before 8 A.M. PDT on that date, I received a telephone call from an aunt in Connecticut asking me if I heard the news. I said that I hadn't turned on the television or the radio since I awoke. She told me that the World Trade Center buildings were no longer standing, having been hit by planes hijacked by terrorists. I thanked her for the call, related the news to my wife, and we both viewed the replay of the events on television. While I watched, I felt an impact of the energy that appeared to be destruction, devastation and death. As I took those labels off, I felt myself resonating with the explosive nature of the energy that kept expanding within me. I had the sensation of soaring like a large bird whose wings were being pushed upward by an enormous flow of loving energy. My heart was filled with gratitude for being the recipient of this wonderful gift.

Listening to the comments of newscasters about the horrendous consequences of the actions of the hijackers, I felt enveloped by the power of the love that had been released in the Universe. Before this event, I was clear that no one dies, there are no victims, and each of us has the precise experiences we have come to the human to have.

However, I quickly became aware that not many years ago, my beliefs included the acceptance of the reality of victims, death and grief. I felt compassion for those whose present experience was not unlike what had been my own. I also saw each of them as the God Presence courageously entering into the fullness of the experiences they came here to have.

There is Nothing Outside of Me

This has been one of the most challenging of the Principles for me to embrace, since I have hidden a lot of my power in playing the role of "victim" in many ways for many years.

Recently, I have had two opportunities to test my willingness to accept the truth of this Principle that I wish to share.

On a morning in April of 1999, I was awakened by an uncomfortable sensation on the right side of my chest. An inspection revealed the presence of lesions starting at the midline on the front and continuing around to the spine on my back. I was told I had contracted what is commonly called "the shingles." The medical term is post-herpetic syndrome, a condition believed to be the result of damage caused by a reawakening of the virus that originally causes chicken pox.

The pain was very intense. First, I tried homeopathic remedies, to no avail. This was followed by an analgesic, with the same result. Several people told me that the pain would probably leave after about two months. I decided to tough it out for that period of time. However, no decrease in the pain level occurred. I realized that it was time for me to see the circumstance as perfect just the way it was.

With the support of my spiritual coach, I began the process of changing my description of what I was experiencing from that of being at the effect of forces outside of me to being the force itself. This meant feeling the fullness of the energy as the Power of God. This was an enormous challenge since my mind insisted on calling the energy "pain." I continued with this process for over two years before my new description of the energy became real for me.

In retrospect, I know how valuable the experience has been. I learned the depth of my commitment to uncover the disguises that hide my power. I also learned that I am able to trust the truth of how powerful I really am even though my experience seems different from that truth.

In the spring of 2001, I noticed termite droppings in two

places around my home. I was surprised to again see a reflection of the belief that something can cause me damage. Then I realized that the droppings were a gift. The gift was the information that although I had opened a lot of energy in the belief that something (a virus) can cause me harm, there was a residue of the belief left.

This led to another gift, the opportunity to remember that I am the God Presence to whom no harm can come. I felt deep appreciation for the support brought by the termites. Since there is nothing outside of me, this is feeling deep appreciation for myself.

CHAPTER 16

⌖

Further Reflections

The Illusion of Conflict

The two most noticeable responses to the events of the morning of September 11, 2001 are:

1. a compassionate reaching out to the families of those whose physical lives ended as a result of the hijackings, and

2. an anger leading to a desire for retaliation against those who supported the hijackers.

The energy in both responses is the same even though they appear on the surface to be vastly different. For there is one energy in the Universe—love—and that is all we are ever experiencing.

The opportunity we have, as we continue on this human journey, is to expand our vision to keep discovering love until all we experience and express is unconditional love and support. The challenging (or fun) part, depending upon how we view it, is feeling love for those people who disguise their actions in ways that seduce us into judging them.

Peace

Although the anger and desire for retaliation has led to aggressive action, there is also a surge in the desire to have this lead to peace. This contravenes the Principle of Means and Ends—the action and the outcome are one. In other words, when we choose to wage war to bring about peace, we end up with more war. The only way we create more peace is by choosing peaceful means.

For those who prefer the challenge of aggressive activities for the excitement it provides, let's compare alternative approaches. There are two parallel continuums. One is the boredom—excitement continuum, the other is the peace—inspiration continuum.

The reason that many people seek the excitement of aggressive activities is that they are looking to overcome boredom. However, when this choice is made, the excitement must continually increase to overcome the boredom that grows at the same rate. This is true since the Universe is in a constant state of expansion. Whatever choice we make, we keep experiencing more of that choice.

What happens when the choice is more peacefulness? Peacefulness is the absence of inner conflict. Inner conflict arises from the choice to hide our power; we set up a tension between the part of us that is naturally peaceful and the disguised part that keeps the power hidden. The result is the creation of the boredom—excitement continuum.

As long as we keep the power hidden, the natural expansion of energy causes the tension to build, intensifying our sense of boredom and thus a craving for more excitement.

When we choose inner peacefulness, we encourage a rise in the level of inspiration. Unlike excitement, which generates tiredness from the effort required to repress the energy, inspiration induces an increased flow of energy. The expression of this energy (love) contributes to greater feelings of peacefulness that in turn stimulates more inspiration. Those who choose the peace—inspiration continuum are drawn to activities that promote harmony, generosity, gratitude and unconditional love leading to abundance and joy.

Free Will

The Universe has gifted all of us free will. There are no bad or wrong choices. Some of us choose to keep our love disguised in beliefs in limitation, powerlessness and death. Others of us choose to feel unconditional love for those who have disguised their love. No choice is better than another. The question we can ask ourselves is: "Which choice feels more enjoyable?" Both choices are equally challenging.

A Remarkable Accomplishment

Our vantage point is always the present state of our consciousness—what we really believe. When we proceed to open these beliefs, we often feel uncomfortable. This is because we intentionally encase many of these beliefs in disagreeable feelings so that we avoid going near them—a very clever device we use to keep our power hidden.

However, we feel discomfort only because we have taught ourselves to believe the energy we have hidden is uncomfortable. In truth, all that we ever see and feel is love.

The process of clearing our consciousness of beliefs that we create to hide our power, peacefulness, harmony, abundance and joy has been set forth in this book. A wonderful way to prepare ourselves for embarking on this process is by feeling deep love and appreciation for ourselves for the remarkable accomplishment of creating the precise lives we are living. And remember, each of us is the Power of God experiencing and expressing in our own unique and perfect way.

The Greatest Gift

The greatest gift the Universe can possibly give to us is the opportunity to love unconditionally; and, each of us has been offered this gift. As part of our brilliant plan to hide our power and the truth of who we are, we create beliefs in the reality of conditions that make it seem almost impossible to even consider accepting the gift: shame, failure, murder, disease and death, to name just a few.

When we are ready to allow the truth of who we are, our Soul Self, to emerge, we begin seeing the conditions as disguises for our power and our love. As our clarity for this worthiness grows, so does our appreciation for the value of this extraordinary gift.

Another exceptional gift we are offered by the Universe is the opportunity to see everything as a reflection of the state of our consciousness. This incredibly accurate feedback, that is always available, allows us to see clearly the beliefs we still accept as reasons to avoid the opportunity to love ourselves unconditionally.

This game we call life is set up for all of us to win the ultimate prize—the opportunity to love unconditionally. The Universe has offered us this gift unconditionally. This means we are deemed worthy of receiving it by being precisely who we are, just the way we are. When we deem ourselves as deserving as the Universe already does, we claim the prize. And we encourage all others to claim the prize by loving them unconditionally just the way they are.

CHAPTER 17

⋋⋌

Spiritual Coaching for People in Business

The benefits I have received from the spiritual coaching process has inspired me to offer that support to others. I have initially been drawn to offer that support to entrepreneurs, owners of their own businesses.

Opening to a New Way of Being in Business

When a person chooses to open a business, one of the first requisites is finding the appropriate physical space. When a person chooses to develop the business and take it to a higher spiritual level, providing the appropriate space for that is just as important.

This is about providing such a special kind of space — one that is loving, nurturing, unconditional and supportive — for you to open into, and for you, in turn, to open for those with whom you interact: employees, associates, customers, suppliers, family and friends.

Every business is a potential playground for all who are involved to have fun playing together in ever more creative and inspiring ways. All the elements are already in place. Once the space is opened, the participants open themselves to new ways of being together.

There is no instructing or trying to make things better. There are no goals set or rules to follow.

Every situation that appears uncomfortable and constricting has within it the information that, when understood, uncovers creativity, inspiration and fun and opens more space. We are masters at hiding what we enjoy and feeling constricted. We are potential masters at finding the hiding places, uncovering the fullness of who we are and opening space. With simple support, that mastery can be developed. You will know when you are ready to open to this gift and appreciate the support that is waiting for you.

CHAPTER 18

੭

Frequently Asked
Questions

Valuing

Question:

I find myself short of money all of the time. I practice frugality, and am very careful what I spend my money on. Do you have any suggestions?

Answer:

We determine the value of everything in our lives. In our money-oriented society, we demonstrate our value assessments by what we pay for, and how much we pay. Many of us have been trained to believe that the less we spend for something the better. Therefore, we often unwittingly place little or no value on things that have great value: teachers who inspire their students, and social workers and nurses who are loving and caring to their clients and patients.

Since we are also trained to believe that our abundance is limited, we diminish our valuations to conform to our perception of diminished capacity to pay. The solution lies in the companion of valuing—appreciation.

Appreciation is the feeling quality that gives value its power and opens the door to our abundance. We are feeling beings and we connect with our power through our feelings. When we allow ourselves to deeply appreciate what we value, we are in closer touch with the abundance that is all around us. We also open ourselves to allow that abundance into our lives.

Thus, we complete the circle. Having decided that something is of great value, we feel appreciation. This opens us to the abundance, which in turn allows us to demonstrate our appreciation for the value we are receiving.

The capacity to feel appreciation is an extraordinary gift that the Universe has bestowed upon us. To take full advantage of this gift, I suggest the following sequence: Feel appreciation for the God Presence, the source of your capacity to feel appreciation. The flow of energy you feel from your connection to and appreciation for this Presence activates your capacity to feel appreciation for yourself. This places you in the perfect position to appreciate everything, and reinforces in your consciousness your Oneness with all that is.

The more we practice feeling appreciation, the more reasons we find to feel appreciation. What is better than a life full of people and things that we appreciate? What is better than opening ourselves to more abundance that is then available to express our appreciation? Practicing appreciation is a gift that expands infinitely in all directions.

Have fun!

Expanding Our Vision

Question:

I have a friend in her early 20s who is suffering from many health problems, and I'm trying to figure out how I can support her?

Answer:

The best way to support her is to see her whole and complete as the God Presence that she really is. She is not her physical body. In order to do this, you first have to see yourself the same way.

As you seek to support your friend, recognize that she is giving you a wonderful gift. Take advantage of this gift, and show your appreciation for the gift by seeing the truth behind the veil of physicality.

Seeing our physicality as though we are simply physical beings is like a dog chasing its tail. When we see our physicality from the vantage point of the God Presence, we appreciate that the physical experiences we have are just a purposeful excursion into self-imposed limitations. When we are ready to expand our vision, the Universe provides us with the perfect support to open to the power we have hidden in our beliefs in limitation.

Expanding our vision means opening ourselves to being the God Presence. Take some time to visualize or feel yourself as more than just a physical presence. When you are in that expanded energy, embrace yourself as a physical being and feel appreciation for the experiences you have had and continue to have as such an entity. Appreciate all the courage it has taken for you to embark on a life of perceived powerlessness and limitation. Feel appreciation for all those people who have supported you in having those experiences. See the continuity in the progression from seeing and feeling life from the vantage point of a physical being to one as the God Presence.

Competition

Question:

My five-year-old son has recently gotten into BMX racing. I'm uncomfortable with the competitiveness of it. Am I going against principle by letting him do it or has he chosen it himself as an experience/ learning tool and it is not about what I think at all?

Answer:

The responses we have to any event or circumstance tells us what we believe about ourselves, and the world around us. Your son's choice of a competitive activity has aroused both doubt and trust in the wisdom of his choice. This tells you about your view of competition.

Competition is neither good nor bad. It is a form of interaction that we may relate to in many different ways. Instead of looking at it in the traditional way, you may see it as an opportunity to express the best that is in you, rather than as a way to be better than another participant.

In fact, you may see the situation as a mutually supportive activity where all participants are really on the same side rather than on opposite sides. If this approach feels good to you, your son will easily pick up on your new view of his activity.

You and your son are in parallel and interwoven universes at the same time. Everything you do, say or feel impacts him just as everything he does, says or feels impacts you.

Each of you is a wonderful support for the other. The more appreciation you feel for him, the more appreciation he will feel for you as well as for himself. The more appreciation you feel for him, the more appreciation you will feel for yourself.

There is so much love to be shared here. Enjoy!

Judgment

Question:

The recurring difficulty I experience while working at releasing judgment is my inability to view things like murder, rape, violence, etc. as just events neither right nor wrong. Using the example of Hitler and the Nazis for instance, how would you suggest I deal with this?

Reply:

Each of us is free to see life any way we wish. If we choose to accept the belief in "right" and "wrong," whatever we judge becomes for us the way we judge it. If I insist on seeing a criminal as a "bad" person, that is the way our relationship unfolds. He will continue to behave in ways that justify my judgment of him.

Our criminal justice system is a perfect example. We judge people we call criminals as "bad" and they keep acting in ways that support our view of them. As a society, this judgment has led us in ever-expanding circles for many years.

As soon as anyone is willing to release a judgment of someone, the energy that is frozen in place by the judgment is freed. All energy is love and we are free to use it in any way that we wish. We can use the energy to support our belief in "right" and "wrong," or we can free it to be loving energy that embraces, nurtures and harmonizes all it touches.

Each of us is the whole of the Universe and all that we see is ourselves. Horror and misfortune are in the eye of the beholder. So are beauty, wonder and magnificence. We are each free to choose in each moment.

Core Beliefs

Question:

My core belief = I'm bad. I felt separated from my parents, since I felt they did not understand me, they didn't understand where I was coming from, and because they were not even interested in how I felt. They seemed only interested in me obeying their every command and to be willing to do things that I didn't enjoy or things I hated, without any talking back. My mother's famous words were "As long as you live under this roof, you will do as I say!" Since my structural belief is that "I'm bad" or selfish, I have difficulty in loving that belief or appreciating it. I think this has been my main problem —I dislike having the "I'm bad" belief so much and I want to look good so much (so others don't see the real me as "bad" as I subconsciously think) that I am willing (reluctantly) to do things I dislike.

Answer:

Thank you for your honesty and your clarity.

First of all, be aware that many people have a core belief similar to yours. Next, remember that you went to great lengths to acquire and experience the core belief, and your parents went to great lengths to support you in acquiring and experiencing the belief.

You are all on the same side even though you perceive that

you are on opposite sides. Taking your parents out of their adversarial role and into a supportive role will go a long way toward opening your energy around this core issue.

As for the core belief, there are really two parts to it. The first is the belief that you are "bad." The second is the belief that you have to be accommodating to people so that they will like you in spite of the fact that you are "bad."

As for opening the energy bound in the belief that you are "bad," the first step is to acknowledge the part of you that has created the belief. Appreciate how clever and resourceful this part of you has been to sell you this untruth.

The second step is to allow yourself to feel all the energy in the belief free of the label "bad." When you are able to feel all that energy, open your heart and feel love for it. This energy is your power. As you do these steps over and over again, you will feel yourself regaining a sense of how powerful you really are.

Remain conscious of your need to please others. Notice how this need weakens as you open the energy around the belief that you are "bad."

Be patient and kind to yourself.

Comment from Questioner:

I sat in on a mutual support group meeting as you suggested. I found the meeting to be very uplifting and supportive. I enjoyed it a lot. What I sense is that if I had a woman in my life that was like those in the mutual support group and also was associated with co-workers of the same supportive nature, it would not matter much at all that I still had the belief that I was bad or selfish. Because even if I wasn't giving fully, the other person whom I would be relating to would still be supportive and understanding and loving in word and deed, in gen-

eral. There wouldn't be much need for me to handle the undesired internal belief.

Response:

What you have stated is again a very common belief. Holding onto this belief is a perfect way to avoid opening the energy that is making you so uncomfortable.

The people in your life are the perfect people to be there. You are all in support of each other. You didn't make any mistake nor did they. No one wandered into each other's life by accident.

If you were to move, change your employment or divorce your wife, you would remain in the same feeling state. The new people in your life would look and feel just like the ones you left.

There is one constant in your life and that is you. As long as you hold onto a belief, you will keep experiencing the out-playing of that belief. You came here to feel love for yourself and all of the other people in your life just the way you all are. You also came here to appreciate them for their remarkable support of you and to appreciate yourself for your willingness to go into these uncomfortable feelings.

There is no way to finesse or do an end run around your purpose for this lifetime. You are right on target. Appreciate yourself for that.

Your awareness has increased immeasurably and will continue to increase as you proceed. And as much as possible, lighten up. You can have fun with this.

Anger

Question:

When I get angry is it really someone else's anger? Someone else is viewing my anger and it's not really mine, it's theirs?

Answer:

You cannot resonate with a feeling unless you have that feeling. If it appears that you are witnessing someone else's anger, and you are able to feel any of it, the anger is a reflection of yours.

You are the whole of the Universe and all that you see is yourself. Turning this around so that you become the mirror rather than the one looking in the mirror is just a way to avoid both accepting how powerful you are, and the support you are being offered.

There is no power in the mirror. The power is in you. However, you have hidden that power in your beliefs. The extraordinary gift you are being offered is the opportunity to see everything as a reflection of those beliefs. Then you may open the energy in the beliefs to reclaim your power.

This power is love—the only energy in the Universe. We give this energy many names including "anger" to give us different kinds of human experiences.

Whenever you have a feeling that you call other than love, see if you can remove the label you have assigned to the feeling and feel the love. The more willing you are to acknowledge that all energy is love, the more joy you will allow into your life.

Question:

When you talk about "opening up the energy around your anger," do you mean that all the experiences that we have in our lives are really just opportunities to experience all sorts of emotions and then move on? For instance, if you get angry over something, do you mean that you should just feel the feeling of anger and that the incident which caused the emotion is irrelevant—just a means to an end? If so, is it pointless to plan your life in order to avoid incidents where negative emotions could be created, e.g., avoiding someone whom you know you always end up in an argument with?

Answer:

When our hearts are open wide, our energy (love) flows freely and we feel joyful. When we wish to experience something other than joyfulness, we close our hearts restricting the flow of energy. One way we can do this is by judging someone's actions as unacceptable.

When we are ready to open the energy in our anger, we broaden our view of the situation. This means acknowledging that we have chosen to create the judgment, and that those participating with us are volunteering their support. When we open our hearts in appreciation for their loving support, we free up the flow of our energy.

We are all very powerful beings who have gone to great lengths to create beliefs that are designed to convince us that we are really powerless, helpless and fearful beings. Our power is in our feelings. Our beliefs act as disguises for our feelings to help us hide this power.

Our natural state is the free flow of love. As our energy, which is love, flows freely, we feel joyful and powerful.

Compare how you are feeling with your natural state. Notice the ways you disguise the energy, such as with feelings that you call anger.

Forgiving Yourself

Question:

I am trying to find a way to forgive myself for something I feel is really horrible. I am a 51 year-old man who about 20 years ago left my wife and kids. At the time I felt it was the best thing to do. I felt overwhelmed with responsibility, angry to an extreme and was physically abusive to my kids. The only contact I have had with them has been in sending them money over the years. After reading your books it sounds like you are saying that the principle of perfection would say that what I did was OK but I can't seem to accept that. I have had these horrible feelings for 20 years and I would like to unload this burden and see how my kids turned out. Do you have any advice?

Answer:

Your focus is absolutely correct. This is about you forgiving yourself. Your belief about your behavior (terrible), and your label for your feelings (horrible) provided you with hiding places for your power that allowed you to have the familial experiences you have had.

Before you came into the human, you intended to create these experiences. Your family members agreed to play the supportive roles. You are all in this together in mutual support.

You have started the process of forgiving yourself. Being clear on the complicity of your family releases them from their roles as victims and frees you of the guilt that precludes your willingness to forgive yourself. The next step in the process is appreciating how courageously the participants in your situation have been performing their roles. This includes you.

There are no mistakes or accidents in the Universe. Everything that happens is purposeful. And, each participant is a volunteer in support of all the other participants.

Following the foregoing suggestions is simpler if you step back from the situation and view it from a broader perspective. Open yourself to see the situation and the participants as part of a divine exploration—a courageous attempt to expand the divine consciousness through the exploration of the human experience. See the participants as who they truly are: the God Presence.

No one can be hurt because you are not separate entities. When you are able to enjoy who you really are, your joy is felt by all who join with you in what you call a human tragedy but is really a human celebration.

You believe that your behavior was "wrong." The belief in "right" and "wrong" is a choice we make to give ourselves the experiences that result from that belief.

Remember, we are all the God Presence. We are not who we make believe we are. We have had to create many contrivances to keep ourselves away from the truth of our real nature, which is to be unconditionally loving. The main vehicle that we all use to give ourselves our human experiences is being judgmental.

As for visiting your children, after you feel forgiveness for yourself, you will sense the perfect time to visit with them.

Death—No One Really Dies

From A Letter:

"... It has been a very rough year ... I lost my two very dear brothers and my lovely sister-in-law within a four month time. It was a very, very troubled time for me. As my husband said, since I love deeply, I hurt deeply ... It is especially hard to see their young children grow up without them ...

... The support from my community when my family members passed was tremendous ... Truly all is well in my world and I have a great life and much to be grateful for ..."

Reply:

The difficulty you are having in accepting the circumstances you describe is understandable. However, there are no accidents or mistakes in the Universe, and you obviously chose to open the energy around what we call "death." In order for the events to appear real, you need others to play the roles that you describe.

No one really dies. Those of us who choose to experience human form give up memory of who we really are, but only temporarily.

As we open the energy in beliefs in how limited and powerless we are, we become aware of how unlimited and powerful we really are. Eventually, we confirm with eyes that see beyond our own dimension that there is no "death," and that those who shared time with us as humans are continuing on their journey just as we are.

Since we are all One, each journey enriches everyone. You have much to be thankful for, as you note in your letter, and your capacity to uncover the joy in all of life is truly unlimited.

You may wish to communicate with those family members who have moved on. My way of connecting is to open my heart and feel deep unconditional love for them, as I feel their deep unconditional love for me. I know they wish the best for me, and I can feel that support. The time I spend in this way is very inspiring and energizing.

Everyone's experiences in life are unique. Trust yourself to give and receive unconditional love without limitations of any kind. And enjoy what happens.

CHAPTER 19

⟡

Universal Principles
(*The Journey* Edition)

Universal Principles are the guidelines that govern our lives perfectly.

1. Energy = *Love*

The basic component of the Universe, energy, occurs in either materialized or unmaterialized form. All that we see and feel is an expression of energy.

Energy is synonymous with love. When we resist the flow of energy, or love, we experience discomfort. When we align with the energy flowing around us, we feel joyful and at peace.

2. Infinite Intelligence, or God

Within all energy is an intelligence that is infinite, eternal and purposeful. This Infinite Intelligence, which we sometimes refer to as God, or simply love, is the source of all creative expression and the essential power in the Universe.

The way we view our Infinite Intelligence, or God, is precisely the way we experience life. When we perceive God as an unconditionally loving and supportive energy at all times and under all circumstances, we experience our world and everyone in it as totally safe, loving and generous.

3. Oneness

Since the essence of everything is pure loving energy, in the truest sense, *we are One*. When we feel our connection to our Oneness, we feel the power of who we really are.

Our Oneness, love, is indivisible. Whenever we attempt to withhold love from anyone, we withhold love from everyone, including ourselves. The truth of this principle becomes clear as we allow our hearts to open and feel our interconnectedness.

4. There Is Nothing Outside Of Us

In order to have our human experiences, we created the apparent reality that we are living outside the Oneness; that there are things and people that can affect us without our consent. The truth is that there is nothing outside of us; all that we see is our Self. This becomes our new reality when we open the belief in separation and accept the truth that we are the Power of God.

5. Perfection

Our Oneness, God, is perfect and expresses this perfection as unconditional love and support. Whatever unfolds is God happening. When we see other than unconditional love unfolding, we are not seeing clearly. We create unclarity to have the experiences that we came into the human to have.

When we are ready to see with greater clarity, we embrace whatever is before us in unconditional love, trusting that the Universe, in Its constant expression of unconditional love, is sending us the perfect support. With practice, our clarity grows, along with our appreciation for the unconditional love and support that is always present.

6. Beliefs

Under the guidance of our Souls, we intentionally adopt the beliefs we hold in order to provide ourselves with the precise experiences we are having. These beliefs help us hide our power so that our journey as humans can unfold as we planned before we entered this realm.

The urge to explore life as a human beyond the limitations of these beliefs is a signal that our Soul Selves are looking to guide us in finding and reclaiming the power we had previously hidden, and to awaken us to the truth of who we really are.

7. Intuition, Feelings and Power

Our Infinite Intelligence communicates to us through our intuition, which we access through our feelings. The more willing we are to feel our feelings, the more able we are to connect with the power that resides in them.

The true power in the Universe is a totally peaceful power. It is the power of love, fully, freely and joyfully felt.

8. Mutual Support

Our Universe functions as a mutual support system in which each and every thing in existence relates to and affects every other thing. Every person and circumstance in our lives is there to support us by reflecting back to us the present state of our consciousness.

The prevalent belief that we are naturally competitive and adversarial is just a mirroring back to us of our acceptance of that belief. The more we look for the support that is present in each event and circumstance in our lives, the more we appreciate how perfect the Universe's support for us truly is.

9. The Mirror Principle

Everything that we see and feel is a reflection of the state of our own consciousness. Every person we attract into our lives is showing us a perception we hold about ourselves. Every feeling expressed by another mirrors a feeling deep within us.

This reflection is a gift, for it allows us to be aware of the beliefs we hold, and the power that we have hidden in them.

10. Nonjudgment

We have been carefully taught to evaluate and judge much of what we experience. However, right and wrong, good and bad are just beliefs, places where we have hidden a lot of our power.

The truth is that everything that occurs is just another event or circumstance. Judging something keeps whatever we judge the way we judge it. Also, judging anyone or anything tells us that we are judging ourselves in the same way.

Judging creates discomfort within us that can only be relieved by opening our hearts, first to the judgment and then to the person or thing we have judged. Expanding this openhearted energy leads to the joyful feeling of unconditional love for ourselves as the wholeness and completeness of who we really are.

11. Purpose

Our Soul knows our purpose for this lifetime and initially supports us by helping us hide our power and our knowing so that we may have the experiences we came here to have. When we are ready to reconnect with our God Presence, our Soul supports us in uncovering our power and our knowing. We are always on purpose, and we are always a God Presence receiving the perfect support for experiencing and expressing ourselves in accordance with our purpose.

12. Comfort and Discomfort

Our bodies are magnificent instruments that we *create* to support us in having the experiences we come to the human to have. Our bodies are created and maintained in consciousness. They mirror the state of our consciousness, which includes the collective consciousness beliefs in how to look, act, age and die.

Unencumbered by our beliefs, our consciousness is unlimited, as are our bodies. The natural state of our consciousness is perfect ease, as is the natural state of our bodies. The limited beliefs we have about our bodies are there to love and embrace just the way they are. This opens the energy held in the beliefs as it opens the energy in our bodies from that of dis-ease to ease.

13. Abundance

Abundance is our natural state as God Presences. Everything we experience is part of the abundance. When limitation appears, we are seeing a reflection of our beliefs in limitation. Opening these beliefs provides us with a clearer view of our abundance.

14. Giving and Receiving

Giving and receiving always occurs in balance. It is as important to receive gratefully, as it is to give voluntarily, generously, and with no expectations. Our willingness to keep the energy flowing in and out of our lives supports the energy in expanding.

The corollary to the principle of giving and receiving is that we give only to ourselves. Since we are all One, when we give to another, we are really giving to ourselves.

15. Nonattachment and Freedom

Our perceived need to hold on to anything or anyone demonstrates our beliefs in shortage and personal incompleteness. Holding on to anything—people or possessions—blocks the flow of energy around our experience with the person or object and reduces the joy of the experience. It also inhibits new people and new things from coming into our lives.

As we open our hearts and expand our trust in the natural abundance of the Universe, we give ourselves and everyone else the gift of freedom.

16. Expressing Who We Really Are

Each of us has one or more talents we love to express. When we are fully and freely expressing who we really are, we feel joyful and fulfilled.

The more love we feel for ourselves, the more we allow the creative energy of the Universe to flow through us. Since how we see and feel about ourselves is how we see and feel about other people, feeling more love for ourselves is the most mutually supportive focus we can have.

17. Means and Ends

Means and ends are the same. The action and outcome are one.

To achieve peace, we feel and express our inner peacefulness. To enjoy a life that works perfectly, we see and feel the perfection of everything and everyone, including ourselves. To experience the natural abundance of the Universe, we feel and express gratitude for everything just the way it is.

18. Harmony in Relationships

Every relationship in our lives reflects our relationship with ourselves. Every person we attract is there to support us in opening our hearts and reclaiming our power.

When we feel love for ourselves, and the perfection of ourselves, just the way we are, we attract loving and harmonious relationships with other people.

19. The Universe Handles the Details

Taking care of the details of our lives is generally considered a rational-mind activity. However, when our rational minds are active, we shut out our Infinite Intelligence, which has the capacity to handle the details in ways that are vastly more supportive of us and everyone else.

As we learn to relinquish our rational thinking and surrender to our intuition—our connection to Infinite Intelligence—we discover how easily, effortlessly and spontaneously events unfold for us.

CHAPTER 20

✧

Meditations from Grady Claire Porter

Morning Focus

I awaken in total trust that everything the Universe brings me in this day is a gift of love and support. I feel deep appreciation for these gifts and I unconditionally accept them all. I see the activities of my day as an experience and expression of my expanded Soul awareness, and I rejoice in all of them, exactly as they are. I feel the abundance bestowed upon me by the Universe, and I joyfully accept all the riches inherent in this day. I am committed to an ever-expanding awareness of who I really am. I am in absolute trust that I am unconditionally loved and supported by the Universe and all in it; and I, in accepting that love and support, express it fully to all I see and interact with.

Grady Claire Porter is a spiritual coach and the author of *Conversations with JC*, volumes I, II and III.

Evening Focus

How grateful I am for all the gifts of this day. Thank you Universe for loving and supporting me so gently and wisely. I feel deep appreciation for my willingness to accept your gifts and I feel blessed by each of them. I rejoice in my expanding awareness of my Soul Self, and in the love and support I receive for this expansion. I rest confidently and comfortably knowing that my human self is now renewed to play some more.

This is the Way I Start My Day

I absolutely adore who I am!

I am totally enchanted with every aspect of my life!

I fully appreciate the richness and support each event of my day brings!

And, I consistently allow myself to feel the Love the Universe showers upon me, and all else, in this beautiful, infinite day!

The Peace Exercise

The Peace Exercise is not just an activity. It is a way of life for you from this point on. It is a way to feel the love you have for each part of yourself that you have not yet been ready to unconditionally accept. It is the red carpet for this planet to move forward into absolute joy and harmony. For I tell you this, as you totally and unconditionally love yourself, at all times and under all circumstances, you *are* the High Joy Vibration. And the power of that enlightens the consciousness of whomever and wherever your love and thought are focused.

There are two things that will alert you to begin the Peace Exercise. First, at any time you feel you wish to change *anything or anyone*, you are giving yourself the opportunity to experience the power of peace. The second is justification. At any time you feel you must justify anything, to yourself or anyone else, you are telling yourself you are ready to practice the power of peace.

Now be clear on this. Change and justification are not bad. The desire to change and justify is not bad. Both simply come into your experience to support you in doing what you love to do —*being the power of peace.*

Peace Exercise

I feel, with unconditional trust, that I am the whole of the Universe, and all that I see is Me.

I feel, at my deepest level, the power of being who I am.

I feel the willingness and the readiness to exercise the power of being who I am.

I feel the gentleness of my own power, and the absolute certainty of knowing that my power is the power of peace.

I feel the conviction and trust of my Self so totally that I no longer need to project anything but absolute and unconditional love.

I feel, in totality, the infinite variety of my beingness.

I feel the warmth and peace of unconditionally loving my own infinite Self.

And, at this deep feeling level, I this moment yield to the power of my Self, totally trusting my unconditional love and support for all of Me, and accept all that I see as the expression and experience of this power.

Exaltation

Since in your language "Invocation" is a plea or prayer for support; and since we are playing at a much higher game of acknowledging, accepting and appreciating everything as omniscient support; and since you are committed to ever expanding your experience and expression of perfection; I give you "Exaltation," a highly intensified sense of well-being and power.

I am in total harmony with the perfection of the Universe.

I absolutely trust that this harmonious perfection acts in, as and through me, precisely as I am in the moment.

I deeply know that the action of this harmonious perfection is the sole operating force in the Universe.

I radically rely on this harmonious perfection to support every moment of my human experience.

I unconditionally experience and express the harmonious perfection of the Universe in every activity of my life.

I exalt in the joyful abundance richly invested in me by the harmonious perfection of the Universe.

And, I gleefully exalt in the extravaganza of unconditional love and support that constantly and consistently surrounds me and all in the Universe.

The Human Experience

The human experience is but an exercise for the Soul to practice Its perfection. It is not a trivial experience, and many a Soul return to it time and again to master the challenges it offers.

You are that Soul, returned to the human, to practice the

perfection of who you truly are. You are that Soul, deeply engrossed in the human, so that your mastery is complete. You are seeing that now.

You are seeing that the events of the human have no real meaning, other than to allow you to experience and accept your mastery. The deep emotional chasms of the human but afford you the opportunity of the deep knowing of your Self. You are seeing that getting involved in the drama of the human events is but the challenge to your Soul Self to remember who you are and why you chose this experience.

We have long shared with each other the concept of human perfection—that it's all perfect, just the way it is. And, the truth of that is evidenced in the creative and magnificent activities you create to practice and experience the reality of your true Self. Let's look at a few:

The Body

In the human, the body represents the identity of an individual, as well as the evidence of its life. No body—no life. You see that this opportunity affords you, the Soul, to experience and practice your eternal manifestation of the infinitely unfolding nature of God, your source. Body size or shape is but a reminder of the formless, powerful energy you are. In the human, you create "norms" or "ideals" around shape and form. Again, what a beautiful and perfect opportunity to express and experience the infinite originality of Self. In the depiction of your creation by God, there is only the recitation of you being made in "God's image" and "Behold, it was very good." In the human, the practice is to look to the manifestation to see what God is like. The practice of the Soul is to look to God to know what the creation truly is.

Financial Affairs

This is one you truly enjoy playing with. In the human, you have adopted what you call "a money-driven society." It takes money to do almost anything, and you have made money a condition for having or experiencing any sense of comfort, security or enjoyment. What a perfect opportunity for the Soul to experience true unconditional love and support. You have always seen a lack of money as somehow a failure on your part to succeed—that you must do something, even in consciousness, to allow money to be a part of your experience. The activity around money is one of the most supportive activities the Soul has in experiencing and expressing Its perfection. One of the most entrenched beliefs set up in the human is that you cannot live without money. And, you have many on the planet acting out that belief. Even more entrenched is the belief that you can solve these peoples' problems with money. I have been attributed as the source of the statement "the poor will always be with you." Well, they will, as long as there is a Soul in the human practicing Its acceptance of full and total abundance. I have said to you, "Money is in total support of you," and it is. Acknowledging, accepting and appreciating your financial affairs, just as they are, opens you to the support of money. Loving, unconditionally, not having money is the activity the Soul creates for Itself. You are that Soul. Your commitment to receive and enjoy bountiful financial abundance is a commitment to loving your current financial abundance just the way it is. You will experience huge amounts of money in your life when money is no longer a condition in your life. You are seeing this; you, as the perfect Soul in the human, are embracing, in deep love and appreciation, all aspects of your financial affairs just as they are. The wealth encountered in that experience is beyond money.

Relationships

Whether you are relating to your family, a spouse, a lover, a pet, the grocery clerk, your relationships provide the Soul with a wealth of perfect opportunities to practice Its wholeness and completeness. In the human, a "perfect" relationship is revered as a blessing and an accomplishment. The Soul accepts any and all relationships as perfect precisely as they are. The Soul views all relationships as supportive and utilizes the activity of them to practice Its perfection. The Soul knows that the perfect relationship is the one It has with Its Source, and It knows that that relationship is infinite, unconditionally loving and supportive. You are that Soul.

We began this meditation on the perfection of the human experience and the support it is constantly and consistently offering you, the perfect Soul. Acknowledge, accept and appreciate each and every activity of your human experience just as it is. It will not change itself, nor allow you to change it. It will remain precisely as it is to give you the opportunity to do what you came here to do—*love it all.*

The Business of Being

You have asked me to speak to you about "business."

In the beginning humans came together to support their existence upon the planet. Gradually as each began to develop and enjoy certain aspects and talents, the joy of contribution to the whole was experienced and expressed.

Then, contribution began to be valued on "better" and "more," and "needless" and "not enough." Thus, when one made a contribution to the whole, another sought to make a "better" contribution—and all began to be judged on the quality of their contributions. This activity of rejecting some contribution in favor of others (you now call this business) evolved into the judgment that permeates the collective consciousness today. So, what is judgment? It is unrequited love—love offered but not accepted.

I wish to remind you that all Souls come to the human experience to play. It is like a game of hide and seek. In order to come to the human, the Soul must hide its omnipotence, omniscience and its ability to unconditionally, nonjudgmentally accept and love everything just the way it is. In order to "be" human, the Soul hides itself in its human experiences. Then, with inexhaustible and unerring support from the Universe, this human begins to seek its Soul. It knows where to look — in the human experiences where it was hidden in the first place.

Each of us chose certain human events and conditions to experience. We made this choice long before we came here. We chose those who would support us in hiding our Soul, and those who would support us in finding it. We carefully outlined the support we wanted from the Universe.

Now, we are at the "seek" part of the game. We look for our nonjudgmental, all powerful, all knowing, all accepting Self. Yet hiding and seeking is not all there is to the game. Remember, when found, there is the race back to home base where we are either "Free" or "It". (That's how I remember the game being played.) And, so it is in our game. When we begin to find our Soulness—our power to love and accept under all conditions and circumstances—we have the opportunity to move our consciousness again to our "home base," our complete and total awareness of the perfection of all things. We don't die to do this. We live to do it.

And, the steps in seeking, finding, and returning to home base are all the same—loving and accepting every event and circumstance in our daily lives just the way they are.

It is the same in the game of business. You look attentively at all those things that you would "change," and you love them, you accept them, you unlock the judgment from around them! As your loving energy meets with the energy of the judgment, there is a fusion of power so beatific that it is felt by everyone and everything in the Universe.

Remember, you're not seeking to overcome judgment. You are finding it to love it, to accept it, to blend your power of unconditional love with its own power of unrequited love, in order to establish in consciousness a home base (a business if you will) of total love and support.

That, my precious one, is the *free* enterprise system.

September 27, 2001

What an opportunity to practice our spiritual knowing!

We are clear that every event in our human experience is a mirror of our own consciousness. We are clear that we create these events to give ourselves the opportunity to look at any limited beliefs we may still be holding in order to open them up to a broader and more expansive view of our true selves.

So, in light of current events, we ask: "How are we terrorizing ourselves?"; "What do we believe is 'outside' ourselves to terrorize us?"; and "How can I be a victim and of whom?"

Webster defines "terror" as "a state of intense fear." If we witnessed what went on in New York, and subsequent events, we can be sure that we hold this limited belief in consciousness in some manner or form. We are still holding the belief that there is an outside force or power that can victimize us.

Now, these events were not created to be fixed. They were not created to be avenged or acted upon in any way. They were created for the sole purpose of giving each of us the opportunity to expand our consciousness of who we truly are. And, who are we? The power and presence of God, right here, right now, experiencing and expressing as ourselves. That is the absolute truth about every living thing in the Universe.

My Guidance tells me that "terror" is a clever disguise that I created to hide the intense unconditional love and trust that is the essence of my Soul being, so that this Soul could play in the human as me. He tells me that in order to play in the human my Soul disguised Itself in limited beliefs so that it could have the fun of first experiencing these beliefs, then of unraveling the disguises to reveal Itself once again. I totally trust my Guidance and believe that we all have given ourselves the opportunity to experience the human from our Soul's awareness.

As we fill our consciousness with the absolute truth of the unconditional love, trust, abundance, beauty, harmony, joy of who we truly are, that is what we experience. As we see the events of our day as the opportunity to expand our awareness and experience of these truths, we appreciate and value these events as gifts from the Universe. As we open to receive these gifts, without judgment, our acceptance deepens our trust of our true Selfhood.

I support myself and each one of you in enthusiastically and exuberantly embracing these opportunities.

Appendix

The Mutual Support Group Handbook

by Arnold M. Patent

and Participants of the Mutual Support Network

Editor's note: This revised edition of the handbook was edited to bring it into alignment with the first edition of *The Journey*.

Commitment to Principle

I pledge myself to celebrate harmony, abundance
and support for everyone,
in a spirit of equality and grounded in commitment,
by living my life according to Principle,
which means unconditionally loving and supporting
myself and others just the way we are,
trusting the Universe as I live
in the moment from my peaceful center,
fully and freely expressing who I really am.

_____

name

_____

date

Contents

The Purpose of the Mutual Support Group

As human beings, our most basic desire is to love and be loved unconditionally. Our natural inclination is to support one another.

However, given our years of training in the competitive adversarial model, we have learned to close our hearts and shut off our feelings, both to ourselves and others. Our beliefs in separation, scarcity and struggle have led us to fear and compete against each other. The result has been increasing discomfort and a growing sense of powerlessness, individually and as a society.

Many of us are now ready and eager to reconnect to our true selves—the powerful beings that we really are—and to assist others in doing the same. In reconnecting to who we are, we connect to our Oneness, which is the source of our power.

> *"There is no one as powerful*
> *as a person who feels*
> *loved and supported."*

—Arnold M. Patent

The purpose of the mutual support group is to provide a safe and nurturing environment in which to practice giving and receiving unconditional love and support, reconnecting with our feelings and reclaiming our power. In such an environment, we learn to express qualities that lead to truly fulfilling lives: inspiration, compassion, trust, openness, generosity, gratitude, humor, playfulness and creativity.

The mutual support group is founded on Universal Principles. These Principles are summarized in Chapter 19. When we follow these Principles, we are guided perfectly in enjoying and expressing the love, peace, harmony and abundance that is our natural state.

The following material can assist you in starting a mutual support group of your own. It takes only two willing people to start a group and the self-love to stay with the process.

Suggested Guidelines for
Support Group Meetings

Be sure to go over the following guidelines with everyone who wants to be part of a support group, and review the guidelines periodically. If there are any guidelines your group wishes to modify, it is suggested that you take the matter up before a meeting rather than during a meeting.

1. Be clear about the purpose for the support group: to create an environment in which to practice unconditional love and mutual support; to assist each other in connecting to our feelings and reclaiming our power; and to expand our level of trust in ourselves, in each other, and in the power of our Oneness.

2. Make the commitment to refrain from discussions and advice giving during the meeting. This is a most significant guideline and one that is often disregarded. Remember that we best support others in their personal empowerment by letting them deal with their unique challenges and discover their own solutions.

3. Agree on a starting time and length of meeting (usually 1 to 2 hours) and honor the agreement.

4. Rotate the meeting site, unless the meeting is held at a public facility, such as a business or community center.

5. Notify someone if you will be late or absent from a meeting.

6. Rotate facilitators.

7. Agree to follow the Support Group Format until all participants are fully familiar with the exercises. Thereafter, adaptations may be made by mutual agreement of the group.

8. Honor the confidentiality of personal matters brought up during meetings.

9. Be clear about participant and guest policies, and take time before meetings to inform new participants and guests about the group guidelines.

10. Support the purpose of the group by gently and lovingly reminding participants when the guidelines are not being observed.

Support Group Format

1. Following brief introductions, choose a facilitator for the meeting, or allow one to emerge spontaneously.

2. Center the energy in the group: hold hands, close eyes, quiet minds, focus awareness on feelings. As you open your eyes, make eye contact with each of the members in the circle before releasing hands.

3. Read the Invocation (p. A11) and, if you wish, the Power of Peace Meditation(p. A12).

4. Offer participants the opportunity to go through the Feeling Exercise (p. A14) or the Self-Reflection Exercise (p. A16).

5. State individual purposes (see p. A19 for explanation)
    Acknowledgment: " (Name) , I love you and support you in feeling inspired by your purpose." (See p. A18 about acknowledgments.)

6. State the group purpose (see p. A21).

7. Read one or two Universal Principles (Chapter 19).

8. Share success stories in applying Universal Principles.
    Acknowledgment: "(Name), we celebrate your success(es)."

9. Take a few moments to feel and express gratitude.
    Acknowledgment: "We feel and expand our gratitude for the gifts of love we receive."

10. The Positive-Reflection Exercise (or a variation) or the Self-Acknowledgment Exercise (see p. A23).

11. (Optional) One-Two-Three Laugh! On the count of three, participants join in spontaneous laughter.

    Laughter is one of the simplest ways to open our energy fields, open our hearts, and release our judgments.

12. Requests for support in consciousness (see p. A25).

    Acknowledgment: "(Name), I love you and support you unconditionally just the way you are in all your power and magnificence."

13. Closing: hold hands, close eyes, allow the group energy to expand. Participants may either bring into consciousness silently or name aloud people to whom they wish to send this loving and supportive energy.

14. Set next meeting. Make announcements.

Note: The sequence of this format may be modified to support the continuity of energy within a particular support group.

The Invocation

At the beginning of each meeting, someone in the group volunteers to read the Invocation. The purpose of the Invocation is to remind participants of the support that is always available and to provide an opportunity to consciously connect with this support. It is also meant to connect participants with the Oneness of which we are all a part. The group is free to modify the Invocation if participants wish and if everyone feels more comfortable with the modifications.

We open to the support of all in the Universe,
including our Infinite Intelligence, the God Presence,
in assisting us in awakening;
in assisting us in opening our hearts,
and inspiring and empowering us to support
each other so that we may all
experience the truth about ourselves.
We ask for support in consciousness
in feeling our connection
with the essence of everyone and everything
in the Universe at all times,
so that we can truly know and feel
We Are One.

The Power of Peace Meditation

The Peace Meditation is a gift from Grady Claire Porter. One person may read the whole meditation, or each participant might read one or two statements. Both readers and listeners are encouraged to connect with each statement at a feeling level.

There are two things that will alert you to begin the Peace Exercise. First, at any time you feel you wish to change *anything or anyone*, you are giving yourself the opportunity to experience the power of peace. The second is justification. At any time you feel you must justify anything, to yourself or anyone else, you are telling yourself you are ready to practice the power of peace.

Now be clear on this. Change and justification are not bad. The desire to change and justify is not bad. Both simply come into your experience to support you in doing what you love to do—*being the power of peace.*

I feel, with unconditional trust, that I am
the whole of the Universe, and all that I see is Me.

I feel, at my deepest level,
the power of being who I am.

I feel the willingness and the readiness
to exercise the power of being who I am.

I feel the gentleness of my own power,
and the absolute certainty of knowing
that my power is the power of peace.

I feel the conviction and trust of my Self so totally
that I no longer need to project anything
but absolute and unconditional love.

I feel, in totality, the infinite variety
of my beingness.

I feel the warmth and peace of
unconditionally loving my own infinite Self.

And, at this deep feeling level,
I this moment yield to the power of my Self,
totally trusting my unconditional love and support
for all of Me, and accept all that I see
as the expression and experience of this power.

The Feeling Exercise

We are feeling beings. Through our feelings, we connect with the God Presence, which is the source of our power, our creativity and our abundance. The Feeling Exercise can assist us in reconnecting to the feelings we have repressed. It is one of the simplest and most direct methods of reclaiming our power.

Try practicing this exercise on a consistent, day-to-day basis, until feeling our feelings fully and freely again becomes our natural way of being.

Close your eyes and scan your body. Notice how you are feeling. Then:

1. *Feel the feeling free of any thoughts you have about it. Feel the energy, the power, in the feeling.*

2. *Feel love for the feeling just the way it is. Feel love for the power in the feeling.*

3. *Feel love for yourself feeling the feeling and feeling the power in the feeling.*

As you begin the process of feeling your feelings free of labels, descriptions or judgments, first notice the energy in the feeling. The energy has a vibration; feel the energy vibrate through your body. Then notice the intensity of the energy as it vibrates through your body. Finally, feel this intensity of energy as power—your own power.

During a support group meeting, the Feeling Exercise may be used in various ways. The group may choose to go through the exercise silently together. One participant may lead several others through the exercise while the rest of the participants send loving support, after which participants switch roles. Or if one participant is experiencing very intense feelings, he or she may ask to be supported by the entire group in going through the Feeling Exercise.

Note: The word "love" has been so misused in our society that some people may have an initial aversion to the word. Let your intuition guide you. You might, for example, replace the word "love" with "compassion" or "acceptance."

The Self-Reflection Exercise

When someone in a support group is experiencing very intense feelings around a particular circumstance or situation and feels the need for greater support from the group, another group member can volunteer to gently and lovingly guide the person through the following 11-step procedure. The other members provide additional support by listening with unconditional love.

The person who volunteers to take a participant through the exercise (it may or may not be the group facilitator) reads the following statements or questions, being sure to allow plenty of time for the participant to respond to each statement.

1. Describe the situation in as few words as you need.

2. Are you willing to let go of your interpretation of this situation as being either bad or wrong?

3. Close your eyes and focus your awareness on how you are feeling ... Can you feel the feeling? Can you feel the energy, the vibration, in the feeling?

4. Can you feel this energy as the Power of God that you are experiencing and expressing?

5. Can you feel love for yourself just the way you are as the Power of God? Are you willing to receive support in feeling love for yourself just the way you are as the Power of God? Can you feel the support coming in?

6 Are you willing to accept that what you are experiencing is a reflection of the state of your own consciousness?

7. If there is someone else or others involved in the situation, can you accept that you invited them to support you in reclaiming your power?

8. Can you see and feel the perfection of what is, just the way it is?

9. Take a few moments to visualize and feel the powerful and loving being that you truly are. Connect this powerful and loving being with the powerful and loving being of everyone involved in the situation.

10. Focusing on your heart, allow this feeling of power and love to expand ... When the power and love has expanded sufficiently, let it embrace the situation and all those involved in the situation, including yourself.

11. Feel deep gratitude for yourself for the ingenuity, resourcefulness and commitment you dedicated to hiding your power so that you could explore the human experiences you came here to have. When you are ready, you may open your eyes. If you wish, you may share any insights that have come to you.

Note: If a person has difficulty with any of the steps, suggest that he or she stay with the feelings, open to support in feeling love for the feelings, and continue with the exercise at a later time.

Acknowledgments

One of the cornerstones of the support group process is the use of acknowledgments to express or to send love and support in a very direct, focused way. The words used are less important than the heart-felt intention behind the words.

After a participant has stated her purpose, shared a success story or asked for support in consciousness, the other members acknowledge the person by sending loving energy to her—through their eyes, hearts and hands—as they make a mutually-agreed-upon declaration of support, such as those suggested in the Support Group Format.

Individual Purposes

In becoming aware of our individual life's purpose, we each connect, at a feeling level, with our unique role in the Universe. The more expansive and inspired our purpose, the more supported and empowered we feel in expressing our full potential.

To begin the process of becoming aware of your purpose, let yourself grow quiet and go through the three steps of the Feeling Exercise. In a state of deep self-love and peacefulness, ask yourself, "What is my purpose for living?"

Allow the answer to come to you. Let it be as expansive as you can imagine. The words you choose need not be flowery or poetic; what is important is how inspired the words make you feel. Also, the simpler your purpose, the more powerful it will be.

Some examples of individual purposes:

- My purpose is living with an open heart.
- I feel and trust the power that I am.
- My purpose is radiating joy.
- My purpose is loving myself unconditionally just the way I am.

In a support group meeting, some participants may have prepared statements of purpose while others may choose to have their purpose come to them in the moment spontaneously. Whichever method is chosen, be aware that your statement of purpose provides the greatest benefit when you connect with it every day, and particularly whenever something is troubling you. As you connect with your purpose, you expand the awareness of your importance in our Universe, and your life takes on a new meaning. When you connect with your purpose, you know that you have found the inspiration that makes your life seem worthwhile.

Your individual purpose will continue to inspire you as you revise it periodically.

Group Purpose

Whenever two or more people choose to join together as a group, one of the first and most essential exercises the participants can take part in is to define their group purpose. In the same way that a person's individual purpose creates the inspiration for her life, the group purpose creates the inspiration for the life of the group.

To arrive at the group purpose, participants join in a short meditation and allow a feeling to emerge from a place of peacefulness and connectedness. Each participant then chooses one word that expresses this feeling: love, joy, peace, commitment, power, harmony, trust, fun, Oneness, etc. From this input, the group develops a simple statement of purpose with which everyone resonates, allowing as much time as necessary to achieve consensus. This may happen in one meeting or it may take several meetings, but be sure to keep this a priority item on the agenda until everyone feels inspired and in alignment with the purpose. The creation of a group purpose that inspires each member is the foundation for the group.

Some examples of group purposes:

- *Joyfully playing together as the God Presence.*
- *Being at peace with what is just the way it is.*
- *Supporting each other in opening to the flow of the Power of God as our abundance.*

As with individual purposes, be sure to revise the group purpose periodically so that it continues to inspire all participants.

Our Group Purpose:

_____

_____

_____

The Positive-Reflection Exercise

Participants focus on one person at a time. In turn, each participant looks the recipient in the eyes and says, "The positive qualities I see in you that you reflect for me are . . ." and completes the statement with several qualities that spontaneously come up, such as kindness, vitality, joyfulness, wisdom. The recipient merely says, "Thank you," and the exercise continues until everyone has had an opportunity to receive recognition from all participants.

Note: Be sure to give each recipient a few moments to take in and feel the effect of these loving words before going on to the next person.

Variations

If there is not enough time to do the full exercise, each participant can recognize just the person to his left, going around the circle to the right. Or the exercise may be shortened by stating just one quality per person.

As another variation—and a most powerful one—bring a mirror into the circle, and let each participant do the Positive-Reflection Exercise eye-to-eye with her or himself.

The Self-Acknowledgment Exercise

One person goes around the circle, acknowledging each participant but using his own name every time. For example, Peter would look at Jill and say, "Peter, I love you and support you unconditionally just the way you are in all your power and magnificence." The exercise continues until everyone has had a turn making this self-acknowledgment to all participants.

Requesting Support in Consciousness

Everything that we see and experience is a projection of our own consciousness. Unencumbered by beliefs, our consciousness expresses our Infinite Intelligence, the God Presence. Asking for support in consciousness is a way of accessing this unconditionally loving part of ourselves. We frame each request in terms of Universal Principles. Some examples:

"I ask for support in consciousness . . .

. . . in fully feeling my feelings, feeling love for my feelings, and feeling love for myself just the way I am."

. . . in knowing that I am the God Presence and fully and freely expressing my unique talents."

. . . in feeling my feelings around shortage, remembering that abundance is our natural state, and feeling gratitude for all that I have."

. . . in generously giving and gratefully receiving love and support."

Additional Exercises

The Daily Five-Minute Support Group

This is a wonderfully supportive activity that can be done by couples, families, and in group living situations. If young children are involved, the words can be modified and simplified to make them more easily understood. The Five-Minute Support Group can also be conducted over the telephone.

Each morning, the members of a household come together to make and acknowledge requests for support. In the evening, they reconvene briefly to share their experiences in light of their requests.

The Mirror Exercise

Because we can never truly love and support another more than we love and support ourselves, the most valuable contribution we can ever make is to love ourselves and to continually deepen our feelings of self-love. The Mirror Exercise, done individually on a daily basis, offers a profoundly simple way to increase our love for ourselves.

Stand or sit in front of a mirror. Look at yourself eye-to-eye. Go through the three steps of the Feeling Exercise. Continue looking at yourself until you feel deep love for yourself. Say, "I love you and support you unconditionally just the way you are in all your power and magnificence" or whatever other words you feel inspired to say.

In the beginning, the reasons not to feel love for yourself will predominate and draw your attention away from your feelings. Keep returning your focus to your feelings and to feeling love for yourself. Consider just a small amount of self-love to be a big accomplishment. Little by little and with persistence, the willingness to feel more love for yourself increases. Your heart does open a little more and you do connect a little more deeply to the love that is your essence.

The Forgiveness Exercise

By practicing forgiveness toward those we have judged or are judging as being unloving, we loosen the attachment of the judgment to the feeling, the energy in the feeling is set free, and that energy is then available to us as pure love.

When we are willing to release our judgments of another, we are in fact releasing our judgments of ourselves. Thus, our willingness to practice forgiveness is truly a gift of self-love.

The following exercise can assist you in feeling forgiveness, and ultimately deep love, for anyone you are ready and willing to forgive. Take your time with each step. Be willing to go through the process as often as necessary until you feel deep love for the person (who is really yourself).

For this exercise, you will want to call on the support of the God Presence.

1. Begin by going through the three steps of the Feeling Exercise.

2. When you feel a sense of peacefulness, self-love and support, bring into your conscious awareness a person for whom you hold strong judgments.

3. *Ask the God Presence to assist you in feeling the feelings that are connected to these judgments. Feel the feelings as deeply as you can.*

4. *Ask the God Presence to assist you in feeling love for these feelings. Allow your heart to open and embrace these feelings.*

5. *Feel deep love for the God Presence.*

6. *Ask the God Presence to assist you in feeling forgiveness for this person. Allow your heart to open as wide as you can.*

7. *Let this feeling of forgiveness expand into deep love for this person. When you are ready, embrace the person in this deeply felt, open-hearted love.*

8. *Feel appreciation for yourself for the lengths you have gone to hide your power in this judgment so that you can have this and other human experiences.*

9. *Feel your connection to the Oneness that you are.*

Note: Both the Mirror Exercise and the Forgiveness Exercise may be used in a Support Group. One person volunteers to guide another through the steps of each exercise while the other participants silently offer their loving support.

The Feeling Exercise, Steps 4-6

After you have practiced the first three steps of the Feeling Exercise so that they have become automatic for you, and you are fully at peace with feeling your feelings just the way they are, you are ready for the advanced phase of the Feeling Exercise. The first three steps are the same. These are followed by:

4. *How would you like to feel? Feel the most wonderful feeling you are ready to feel.*

5. *Feel love for this feeling. Feel love for the energy, the power, in the feeling.*

6. *Feel love for yourself feeling this feeling. Feel love for yourself feeling the power in the feeling.*

Note: The power in your feelings can only be accessed by your willingness to feel your feelings just the way they are. Prematurely doing Steps 4-6 of the Feeling Exercise may result in a superficial connection with your feelings, which will keep you separated from your true power. As with all aspects of this work, your honesty with yourself is important.

Background and Support Group Materials

Mutual support groups, based on Universal Principles, have been in existence since 1981. These groups meet weekly in towns and cities throughout the world.

The founder of these groups is Arnold M. Patent. After 25 years of practicing traditional law and attempting to reach harmonious and peaceful results, Mr. Patent turned his attention to practicing Universal Law, a system based on principles of harmony and peace. During this latter career, he has led seminars and written books on Universal Principles.

Mr. Patent's current focus is on spiritual coaching. The basis for this coaching is covered in *The Journey*, which describes his personal experience with the process he uses.

Arnold has also written, *You Can Have It All, Money and Beyond, Bridges To Reality* and a children's book, *The Treasure Hunt*.

He has a website (www.arnoldpatent.com) on which he answers questions submitted by viewers. He is happy to answer any questions that you may have.

69 circle of money
96 the game of hide + seek
44 ✗ ✗ ✗

Printed in the United States
61184LVS00004B

9 780970 808110